Detonation

R. J. Keeler

RESOURCE *Publications* · Eugene, Oregon

DETONATION

Resource Publications
An Imprint of Wipf and Stock Publishers
199 W. 8th Ave., Suite 3
Eugene, OR 97401

www.wipfandstock.com

PAPERBACK ISBN: 978-1-7252-5704-7
HARDCOVER ISBN: 978-1-7252-5705-4
EBOOK ISBN: 978-1-7252-5706-1

Inset cover photograph is from The Edgerton Digital Collections project at MIT. It is an image of the first microseconds of an atomic explosion, documented in a 1/100,000,000-of-a-second exposure, taken from seven miles away with a lens ten feet long. Photographed by Harold Edgerton and his colleagues at EG&G [Harold Edgerton, Kenneth Germeshausen, and Herbert Grier], likely at the Nevada Proving Grounds, on commission for the Atomic Energy Commission; circa 1952. Used by permission.

The Silver Dolphins image is copied from: https://www.public.navy.mil/bupers-npc/support/uniforms/uniformre

The Vietnam Service Medal ribbon is copied from: https://www.afpc.af.mil/Recognition/Decorations-and-Ribbons/

Manufactured in the U.S.A.   12/31/19

Please order additional copies of this book from your local bookstore, not from Amazon—they devour small bookstores. As a last resort to order, send an email to detonation@alumni.duke.edu

Detonation

Miriam,

Regards & love

Rob K

For Isadora Paradise

Contents

Acknowledgements | xi

Abbreviations | xiii

First Part: Love, et al.

Carthage, a Salted Plain | 3

Minotaur at My Door | 4

A Shark Is Not | 5

My Son Jordan | 6

Treechild | 7

In Bed with the Werewolf | 8

Amazonia | 9

The Animal Communicator | 10

God in Underwear | 13

Amour in the Age of Viruses, Porcupines, of Immunology | 15

Voluntarism | 16

A *Verso* Likeness (Imagined, of Course) of Some Acquaintances:
a Childless, Wanting Couple in Aberdeen with Doubt like Water | 17

Black Dirt | 18

Constancy of Method | 19

Gravity: It Must Be Good for Something | 20

The Weather Inside of Us | 21

The Universe is Simply a Sounding Drum | 22

My Heart's Gone Uzi | 24

At the Self-Serve | 25

The Christmas Concert on Orcas Island at Victorian Valley Chapel | 26

Karen's Poem | 27

Trade (Among the Equilibrists) | 28

On Online Dating | 29

Pantoum: Meditation While Washing Laundry | 31

Trophy | 32

Woman Marries Iguana, Carries Eggs | 33

To Lorna Doone from Her Husband, John, after Twenty Years
of Marriage | 34

Second Part: Death

Mud Dauber Wasp Nest | 37

In a Hostage Situation: A Play in Four Acts | 38

Male Sperm Counts Are Falling All Across the Western World | 40

After Chopping off Dozens of Mouses' Heads Suddenly
We Understood Literature | 41

The Altar Fires | 43

Fatherland | 44

Circling on the Edge of the War Zone | 45

Dirty Dead Prick Fish | 46

Strait of Georgia | 47

After a Train There'd Be a Fit | 48

Were We Really So Happy Back Then? | 49

The Literal Mind Was Crushed | 50

Meditation on a Trash Fire in My Backyard | 51

And Pity Those Who Lost Their Grip | 52

On the Earth of Lincoln County, Washington,
on Saint Valentine's Day, 1993 | 53

Along the Shore | 55

Death Is Pique | 56

Eridanus, Mythical River | 57

Assemblage: On a South Dakota Chain Gang in Autumn, 1958
—Air, Ants, and Fervid Thinking | 58

My Transuranium Goblet | 59

Kids Just Getting off the Ferry | 60

Third Part: Literature

Pressure Changes at Snow Lines | 63

A Bee in Late October | 64

A Young Flemish Scientist in Early Contemplation of Gravity
and Light | 65

Hive | 66

The Orb Weaver | 67

A Compass Only Spins That Finds No Source | 69

The Pale Wall Became the Mind Itself | 70

Rue, Herb of Grace | 71

Year of the Gnat | 72

The Cow That Makes Cream | 73

A Puzzle on the Table inside M.V. *Chetzemoka* Underway | 74

Final Canticle, on the Tools for Cultivation of Our Own
Secret Garden | 75

π Covered in Whipped Cream | 76

Symmetry | 78

Fourth Part: Everything Else

White, Black | 87

Flash of Beauty | 88

House of Lords, Temporal and Spiritual | 89

Invasive Species | 90

Curious George and the Man with the Yellow Hat | 91

Inventing a New Color | 92

The Empty Quarter | 93

The Standard Model | 95

A Community of Whores | 98

Window Sitter | 99

And Just This Far from Hopelessness | 102

Anticline | 103

What Do Cats Contribute Positively to Universal Ecology? | 105

Underworld Children | 106

The Woman Who Never Slept | 107

Notes | 109

About the Author | 112

Acknowledgements

I would like to thank the editors of the following journals, presses, and contests who first printed or selected these poems:

- *Alternating Current*: "Trade"
- *Atlanta Review*: "Meditation on a Trash Fire in My Backyard," a finalist for their 2019 International Poetry Competition and published in the Fall/Winter Issue
- *Big Pond Rumours Press*: "A Shark Is Not," "Gravity: It Must Be Good for Something," and "A Puzzle on the Table inside M.V. *Chetzemoka* Underway"
- *Curating Alexandria*: "Window Sitter"
- *Deluge Literary and Arts Journal*: "Carthage, A Salted Plain"
- *Foliate Oak Literary Magazine*: "The Cow That Makes Cream"
- Francis Ponge Prize for Prose Poetry (runner-up): "The Animal Communicator"
- Frost Farm Prize for Metrical Poetry (finalist): "On the Earth of Lincoln County, Washington on Saint Valentine's Day"
- *Garfield Lake Review*: "At the Self-Serve"
- *Helen Schaible International Sonnet Contest, Poets & Patrons of Chicago*: "Male Sperm Counts Are Falling All Across the Western World," Modern Sonnet Contest Special Recognition
- *Jerry Jazz Musician*: "The Empty Quarter"
- *Mingled Voices 4: International Proverse Poetry Prize Anthology 2019*: "Invasive Species"
- *Mithila Review*: "Mud Dauber Wasp Nest"
- National Poetry Library in London (archived): "The Animal Communicator"
- *New Times Magazine*: "Circling on the Edge of the War Zone"
- *Orbis International Journal*: "A Young Flemish Scientist in Early Contemplation of Gravity and Light"
- *PCC Inscape Magazine*: "The Christmas Concert on Orcas Island"

- *Ploughshares*: "Pantoum: Meditation While Washing Laundry" and "The Literal Mind Was Crushed"
- *Prelude*: "The Orb Weaver"
- *Soliloquies Anthology*: "Along the Shore"
- *SUNBEAMS: The Joan Ramseyer Memorial Poetry Contest Anthology*: "To Lorna Doone from Her Husband, John, after Twenty Years of Marriage"
- *The Disappointed Housewife*: "On the Earth of Lincoln County, Washington on Saint Valentine's Day" and was nominated for a 2020 Pushcart Prize
- *The Disappointed Housewife*: "Male Sperm Counts Are Falling All Across the Western World"
- *The Wallace Stevens Journal*: "The Pale Wall Became the Mind Itself"
- *The Poetry Society* (online) "The Animal Communicator," winner of the Waltham Forest Poetry Competition; also nominated for The Forward Prize for Best Single Poem (UK).
- *The Raw Art Review*: "Final Canticle, on the Tools for Cultivation of Our Own Secret Garden," "The Animal Communicator," and "The Standard Model"; all also nominated for the Pushcart Prize, 2019.
- *Tulip Tree Publishing*, Stories That Need to Be Told Contest (semi-finalist): "Assemblage: On a South Dakota Chain Gang in Autumn, 1958—Air, Ants, and Fervid Thinking"
- *Typishly*: "God in Underwear," also nominated for the 2019 Pushcart Prize.
- *Vashon-Maury Island Beachcomber*: "The Pale Wall Became the Mind Itself"
- *White Stag Publishing*: "Rue, Herb of Grace"
- Writer's Digest Writing Competition: "Pressure Changes at Snow Lines," selected for Second Place in the Non-Rhyming Poetry category

Thanks to a long line of teachers, mentors, and fellow students, including Guy Owen, Jim Heynen, Jana Harris, David Wagoner, David Whyte, Matt Briggs, Belle Randall, Richard Kenney, Linda Bierds, Christianne Balk, Jan Wallace, Jane Hirshfield, Nikolai Popov, Susan Lynch, and most especially Heather McHugh.

This work is inspired in part by the late poet John Lawrence Ashbery, who wished his work to be accessible to as many people as possible—and not to be in a private dialogue with himself.

Abbreviations

EG&G	Harold Edgerton, Kenneth Germeshausen, and Herbert Grier
K.L.K	Kathy Lee Keeler
LSD	the psychedelic drug
BS, MS, MBA	standard academic titles
SS	submarine qualified
SSE	south-southeast
IEEE	Institute of Electrical and Electronics Engineers
AAAS	American Association for the Advancement of Science

FIRST PART: Love, et al.

Carthage, a Salted Plain

When he came out of me, he took most of my heart.
Fresh, he tore it loose from its mooring.
His broadside cannonade in flight formed
Cupid's harpoon.
Rammed it into my belly.
Drew me gently back alongside.
Stripped away my innocence in layered spirals.
His dreams bloodied my pelt.

I recall now my sister's oldest name.

Minotaur at My Door

—After Picasso's *Guernica*

I am not afraid, although perhaps I should be:
a killer is loose, hungry for yet another virgin,
and I—not untouched, but still *somewhat* intact;
a bull in heat dreams only of labia and labyrinths.

A Minotaur at my door, hungry for a third virgin,
but boxed in—neutered by luscious, high hedgerows.
When old, he shall always dream of softer labyrinths.
But was I, still a maiden, led into one once? Unclear.

Lonely, hungry, condemned to death—first a hedgerow,
then a cinder path, then low bellowing 'round a corner—
a shock: *I'm here to see—whom? Will he be—clear?*
Now a knock at my door—OK, here, take *my* daughter.

A bloody patch, hot bellowing behind the next corner;
I, way in the past, immaculate. Or—ah, vaguely virginal?
Damn bull's knocking! Oh, my daughter's *not* a virgin?
Not much of me left down *there*, so no fear. Or, should I?

A Shark Is Not

a considerate lover.
Once established, it follows: no shark is an island either.
A shark is not bidden by circumference, but by diameter.
Not tacit; indeed, a shark is wholly inclusive by nature.
Not unprovable, not incomplete; no shark, however algebraic,
    suits God's exemplar.
No shark discounts the Marlboro Man's allure.

Whether a shark is pristine or not remains undecidable, but this much is
    clear: a shark exacts stature.

A shark is neither robot nor bottom-feeder nor agent nor volunteer.
A shark is a matter of kind, not degree.
A shark in the parlor presupposes *haute couture.*

No shark can ever be greater than 1.4 $M_\odot$, posited the self-taught Indian
    astrophysicist Subrahmanyan Chandrasekhar.
Otherwise, it will degenerate into a black hole—which, of course,
    is totally obscure.

When, in the brilliant flash at Trinity, he saw expressed for a tiny instant
    the purple face
    of a shark, J. Robert Oppenheimer,
quoting from the Bhagavad Gita, sang out to General Leslie Groves,
    I have seen Death, the Destroyer.

A woman without a man is like a shark without a bicycle, feminists aver.
All the sharks in Lake Wobegon are above average, quips
    Garrison Keillor.

And thus, in sum, the claim—*quod erat demonstrandum*—is affirmed:
    a shark is not science, but art.

My Son Jordan

Jordan, my son, last hour
your father drove away to
the bus station with you.

We watched you pack
your yearbook, your photo
album. You were so young.

So far away—will you call?
I gave your father our cash
for you. If you need, please. . . .

Next Tuesday's your birthday;
Jordan, what can I get for you?
I'll mail it—just tell me where.

Treechild

Wise Treechild embraces his maternal Yggdrasil,
his sacred World Tree; just as, deep, far beneath
lazy ants, her third root pierces that mythic well
Mímisbrunnr—muddy waters of wisdom and truth.

At dark, Yggdrasil lofts Treechild high up to the sky;
and happily, he feels light, swung to a high journey.

Once aloft, apart thick tangles at last he slumbers.
Gold, lava, puce—writhing serpents wreathe my orbit.
My flesh inherits, knee to neck, swirling waters.
Pay attention, seek connection! their subtle chorus.

Enjoined, he covets Mímisbrunnr's watery quotient,
but Yggdrasil nixes it—her deep well's arrantly nocent.

Treechild chafes—Yggdrasil thwarts his green thirsts?
Ah, slyly he coaxes vexed locusts to her leafy turret.

In Bed with the Werewolf

In bed with the werewolf, which is actually a manwolf
(or, best, womanwolf).
You could
think about a long, bushy tail—soft
and like mother's hair. And a wet mouth, warm
as the broad stones lying in some southern plaza after sundown.

Or curly hair that runs
through fingers like
strong river water through piles of boulders.
Curly hair over muscular flanks.

You could also imagine growling and fear, ripped
throats, gore.

This is really about imagination.
There are no werewolves.

Amazonia

The river spoke longingly of its love of the land.
But the land was stiffer, it stuck up above.

Older and stiffer, from superior strand.
Still, its high mountains had blossoms that year.

I'm fond of your banks, the weight of your hills.
Let me come nearer, said the river to the land.

The Animal Communicator

We have no hope and yet
we live in longing. . . .

—Dante Alighieri, *The Divine Comedy*

I. The Animal Communicator Lets in the Day

As a small flock of maybe fifteen or twenty shrikes
sweeps into and rests among the slick branches
of her Orcas Island backyard pear tree,
her shoulders sag.

II. The Animal Communicator Discourses with a Startled Mountain Lion in the Pasayten Wilderness Just North and East of Sunny Pass

Nothing animal is foreign to me, he murmurs. Still,
she does not drop the clover and lupine she picked
along the path that afternoon; instead holds them
across her right breast.

III. The Animal Communicator Speaks for Herself

Sometimes, after I was born, I wake up in this dream
where I am stalking myself to take back
and bury all the words I ever
spoke or sang.

IV. The Animal Communicator Spills the Word Death

Animals see death differently than we do, she says.
We think of the camp cat that, in 1949, in Bella Vista,
my brother Skip and I pulled entirely apart.

V. The Animal Communicator Gets Down and Dirty

Now you're really going to get it, she says,
as she puts on her headphones
and flips *Start* and *Loud*
on Béla Bartók.

VI. The Animal Communicator Gets Lost in a Rainforest on Bataan

A delegation of walking sticks, golden-fronted leafbirds, lizards,
leaches, lemurs, moreporks, fig wasps, boars, shrews, tarsiers,
vespertilionids, palm civets, anoas, and gray-crowned
scimitar-babblers finds the Animal Communicator
and leads her back deeper into the center
of their own wild moistness.

VII. The Animal Communicator as Sensuoust

Hail had broken scores of panes above the Frontenac hothouse that weeknight.
Before we entered to exhume the orchids, she stripped to the waist
to catch on her belly and arms and areolae
the mixture of green pollen
and bitter snowflakes.

VIII. The Animal Communicator Daydreams of Sex

Toothless and densely furred, an anteater quivers
tucked inside a dream of roe tricked
from within a coveted nest
in the Brazilian backlands
of the Pantanal.

IX. The Animal Communicator Loses Hope

Three lazy, white-cheeked cormorants circle up
into the cumulus over Hat Island
to feed their dry eyes
on vapor.

X. The Animal Communicator Plays God

She lifts her titanium ultralight off well before
dawn and flies side-to-side then end-to-end
above the Grand Canyon until she hits
the first brilliant blue.

God in Underwear

A Careerist in Wonderbra,
everywhere She looked hung
Her sparkling, floating fruits.
Coolly inclined, yet fleet in coltish
air—no union shop.

Her ruby throne floats aloft
the nascent void. Below,
a tribe of naked, scrappy, sweating
cherubs inscribes Her word,
remands to forge a fusty pair
of virgin, sapphire tablets.

No, not a day for thongs—
Day Five coming fast,
She wants to look Her best. She pokes
around a lingerie chest,
lifts a pale-yellow chiffon
pair of Carine Gilsón
knickers up to newly blinding
light, remarks the pair,
and runs a finger all around
the slinky satin hem.

Smooth, bare, left leg first,
then braced by solid throne,
slides the other apiece chiffon;
snaps the seamless top
around an immaculate, untrammeled
waist. Guess no covert
eyes around to glance; She'd squash
them *verso* down to tart,
to something resembling smoky quartz.

Beat was good now;
humming along, She dons a perfect
printed gingham frock,
flicks swarms of fishy things
about, sends fowls off
to chance a pallid, neutral air.

But, oh god, must She now
go on to Man, or may She punt?

Amour in the Age of Viruses, Porcupines, of Immunology

Sans empathy—contempt. At the far side of riverbends
there is quick movement. Could be *wild* pathogens
there *priming* a human immune system? Singularly
brokenhearted viruses abound, *do* carry on famously.

Immune systems for love, for hearts, in hot demand!
Crossed fingers, nixed dreams, or ethical garlic bands
forestall tragedies and unguarded hiccups; all *Hathor*
demands is lechery up and down her lacquered halls.

Is her lover's stolen moon still there if she's not looking?
Neil Bohr's *Copenhagen School of Romance* mistook
his pointing finger for an ersatz, orbiting, half-lit sphere.
No worry, convergent evolutions remand all veneers.

Urania and Melpomene stop by, stick their wet tongues
in your ear, whisper, *Trial and error invite our hot charms.*
Form is ascendant and singular; go step on cracks. Teddy
Roosevelt ate carjacks drenched in cultural multi-psalms.

Curry favor, get a fish to ride a bicycle—or, slash tires,
train as a diesel mechanic, an itinerant knife-sharpener.
Or weigh out a pound or two of gutted Norwegian eels.
Porcupines *do* prime against existential retroviruses.

Voluntarism

Not even use a condom—utter ass!
Forgive you? Never, never. Idiot, jerk.
You knew the risk. Go take your stinking dick,
pound it flat, she said.
                              I didn't know,
he said, *I only kissed him twice.*
                                        Liar!
OK, I only boffed him twice!

She raised and pressed a fist between her eyes.

I always gave you what you wanted. Ass,
my mouth—, she caught her voice. *Oh, why a boy?*
You've killed us both. Our girls—my girls, your girls.
So much undone. You should have thought of them.
I'll never see them graduate or marry.

They circled right a step and stopped. He said,
You'll have to tell them not to use your Schick.

A *Verso* Likeness (Imagined, of Course) of Some Acquaintances:
a Childless, Wanting Couple in Aberdeen with Doubt like Water

On Sundays at three, drinking green Jamaican tea with milk
Respectful and attentive to parents
Correct in approach, conscious of feeling
Patient, conspiring together under covers against the morning clock
Then redolent on the graveled driveway by Mondays at eight
Tennis, poker, the occasional rappel
Careful; monthly rectifying the securities
Clucking at parties at gossip of discriminate fornication

Kitchen table with brochures (*See the Titanic Underwater!*)
In a year, off to Dubai for three months to supervise, then Paris
Half-lugubrious at the cat's death by bicycle
Outgoing, colorful, exploring Tantric

Both constant to their daily journaling
She, with a flair for *juven a la foenta* with Spanish mustard
He, convincing and present among doctors; both, lightships
    to dour professionals
Lovers easily on winter afternoons—perfection of lust

On Saturdays, with a copy of Negroponte, cataloging the city's buildings

Black Dirt

I am not widely known, thus hunt alone,
But bank to run my leeward tacks
And paw moist, dark, illiterate dirt
And ford some interglacial gulch.

Hell, I hum Jacques Brel's *chansons de geste*
To phantom Krell on Altair IV.
Then, rising off the northeast wind, to soar
And crack my talons, kindling dust.

My cat-like interests at our pinkish sun,
Its million million points of light;
A ruche along my felted collar's folds;
My chlorophyll bloods boil and chafe.

I am not widely known, thus mate askance.
Deep in dark dirt my brood's at term.

Constancy of Method

Great egret wing darkens quarter moon,
goes on.
Grey neck breaks night air's symmetry.

All quarters dark or light tug at wings.
Catching and falling, catching and falling,
I must hear still wind fold over wing.

Bright moon, I whisper your fullness.
One quarter bears bright witness,
dark quarters humanize my otherwise life.

Mirror for mirrors, thank you.
Catching and falling, catching and falling,
preserving yourself as an asset.

Gravity: It Must Be Good for Something

Your concentric spheres hum;
     like an oiled bank-vault tumbler,
they click right into place.
But our gravitational attraction,
     so action-at-a-distance,
so Newtonian, so passé—
     drag us away, please, from that so-sheltered era.

I have been torn enough apart
     by transitioning through your event horizons.
So, go wave your silky multi-colorful scarfs—
     then mmmm!—make our joint spacetimes ripple and twist.

Your weak interactions tickle my under-quarks.
All around me my sparse tensors prickle.
Slow, like a lone insect sliding down into a tropical pitcher-plant,
     I glide down your spinning
          torqued-up, neutron-star body.

We dance there.
Gravitonic waves lash us together.
We renormalize.
We interchange our hottest photons.
We settle down to dote on each other.

The Weather Inside of Us

After so much great pain, hope becomes damp.

I love you, she says, but looking at her—at her eyes—
    I see bolts of stark, white energy.

I loathe you, he says, but his tongue forks out
    in jagged repeated rivers. Strident songs
    are unheard—go unnoticed, unrepeated.

We sing about joyfulness but not follow through
    and only brazen horseshit saves us. Emotions
    if inside act like blazing facts, but sadly
    not like facts of ancient pygmy agoras.

Then, before we can say *Snap*, we are both
    standing out on the ledge of desperation. Inside,
    hope and peace mock us—undermine us—
    but faintly, unusually overtopped by half a turd.

What is changing inside, obscured by our generous working surfaces?

What if every shifting thing inside were condensed
    to great mackerel clouds, Hopkins-like thunder,
    mid-gut complications, all kinds of knots and scrapes,
    palliatives and internal swimming loaches, and *Cypriniformes*?

So now he paraglides down between staunch vertebrae,
    while she ski-jumps across thumping adrenal glands.
Snow drifts down, but is it snow or milk of magnesia?

So much empty room inside, they could form up, one-
    on-one, to ex-communicate, then disperse.

The Universe is Simply a Sounding Drum
—James Baldwin, *The New Yorker*, November 17, 1962

Across all our lands strange rhythms fall.
A miserable stardust shifts across and around;
like ocean waves, all quanta go on, unending.

Is this a burning message or just a jam session?
If a message, who may ever read it?
If a jam session—then please, max volume!

Mistah Kurtz, he awoke to pounding:
The drums—The drums, he moaned quietly,
but Marlowe hears only breaking waves.

Who's caused this uproar—the Lilliputians
out on Beta Tau 23, or on some back star-lot?
Or simply a grooved-out, heavy-metal group?

A huge divide slides into weakness.
Then, ribs crack open wide to expose
an irregular but on-beating heart.

Each beat a solidly outgoing signal—
Everything's all right, all things are right;
no cracks overseen in *this* façade,

no failures upcoming for a downfall.
But guts spill all over the teak deck
and fish gills wave in their thin air

and corneas fade to deep translucence.
Where *is* this universe's life force going?
Is it time, after fourteen billion years;

is that old dog finally on her last legs?
Should we think about *the* vet appointment?
Here we've sent robots into vast reaches,

they all seem to report back healthy signs of life.
Light of sorts streaming every direction at once—
it must be going somewhere, no cosmic dustbin

to sweep things up to a tiny, blue glow-ball.
Are gendered universes just palpating each other?
White-hole galaxies move in and out to say it all:

Happiness is at stake if gods forsake our universe.
The sleeping dog on the mat flecks her soft ear.
What she dreams about may indeed matter;

is it about chasing balls or cats or what?
The dog's big, friendly heart pounds—
she simply loves the youngest daughter.

That dog-love swells and quivers
as does any robin's or any salamander's;
no cocksureness here—only a sounding drum.

When that drumskin splits into shreds,
how do we, or not, then send love
to each and every still-trilling architecture?

Some contest or breakthrough pounds out;
time for a universal coffee break to let
the moving, scattered pieces spin to a halt.

Walk on over to the other side, hear ripples' song.
Canard upon canard come together, filament-like;
suns' rumps stick out to bump each other, in secret.

My Heart's Gone Uzi

// because i can still draw a solid bead on your old / too-folly heart /
and crash around / if i could worm myself inside / would you let me in /
to maybe conspire / to pump up the cause // i could bail and bail / i could /
move us along / your gun and mine could go rat-a-tat-tat together /

// if things got too hot inside / we might exchange some ammo clips /
trigger-guards / night 'scopes / or those same seal-team-six-like /
rifle slings // we'd cautiously eye each other across our opposite/
ventricles / mil-dot reticles sending us an exact range to those pulsing /

/ atriums // but i am always closer to you than you to me // you so embody /
zeno's paradox / you move halfway and halfway / and move again in each /
perpetuity / but you never manage to get closer to me // your ethereal but /
so unfriendly stare / at best you blow me a soft wet kiss // i long to close /

/ our distance / to rub out the space where / portmanteau-like / you once /
sat / to grapple your still-folly heart over to mine // that is a sine qua non //
my rifle-safe should be safe lodging to keep your breaths under wraps /
until we can consummate their sensitive gravities // our sights should mix /

/ in revolt / but / should we carousel around the other / shell casings would /
go flying in all elliptical directions / gun-smoke jetting out our separate /
earlobes / volley after volley ensuing like napoleonic wars / tattering our purple /
rainbow auras // i would send my tracers / like ww ii ack-acks / like red- /

/ poppy air-bursts / making you dodge and weave until you / slightly /
imbalanced / reached out to catch yourself / and fell into my singing black /
hole // i'd capture you / as theory holds / untemporarily // we'd disappear from /
all human sight / no more war-torn misinformation leaking out // hawking /

/ could be our best man / we'd circle and circle / within his horizon / our to-be /
vows // but you grab your patent uzi like a snazzy ice skater / pull it in closer /
we instantly speed up // what would you do / in spite or in concert / break our /
one-sided engagement / or belatedly decide to send me my valentine's gift /

/ you had purchased last sestina /

24

At the Self-Serve

Tonight, across the next island, I noticed a middle-age man
crying as he pumped gas into a shiny white, spattered car.

A dull alloy nozzle weighed down his ringed left hand;
a dull-black hose snaked above his invisible knees.

As he stared sideways at the double-timing counter
soft ununnilium light twinkled up his right cheek.

Inside the gasoline dispenser, some imbalance went *umpa*-pump,
umpa-pump. Then on every second beat, some bent gear went s*kreeek*.

After he had driven away, I wondered:
had he been pumping regular?

The Christmas Concert on Orcas Island
at Victorian Valley Chapel

This ovarian island comforted ice
after Polaris sank and Archer followed.
This glacier's ice, many large-fish thick,
lay black and silent in tented hollows.

Then slowly homeward trudged
our sun, that glacier's executioner;
it flinched and shot its warmth, let
ice recede, let flower and sky concur—

a moss that cradled snow now's home
to melting song. Inside this tiny church
a dozen candles flickered toward
the narrow, crowded, public bench

on which we sat—as when my mate
comes home and leaves her tired, ur-
ban creature outside the door. We sang
tonight about a simple gift of myrrh.

Above a cold and remnant mist,
brilliant stars—unseen, unbidden—
blink and shuffle as *Ave Maria* signs
all we commoners suffer hidden:

our brightest fears, our darkest hopes.

Karen's Poem

—K.L.K, in memoriam

Somewhere
between myself at six
and my niece now
I stutter.
Hoping to see her as she will be later,
helped by me as I was then,
seen by me as I am now;
scared.
The power to form in us.

Trade (Among the Equilibrists)
—For John Crowe Ransom

Open systems promote gross imbalance;
promote tariffs, barriers, costs, inequities;
but sadly, blossom into prolific existence.

Closed systems, those rare models of efficiency,
forge chains within chains, forge conservations
between basic parts of self—no profligacy.

Trade for countertrade, action for reaction,
when all is cleared away, the market
captures all extant desires. Encompassing vision

observes all that will be at parity. A deficit
marked down at Jenny's birth zeros a cycle
begun at the quiet death of a tired, old, unfit

West Indian fisherman last year. Treacle
for a white male system's limited, non-
connected, hierarchical view—recycle

old polemics, affirm instead striking notions:
all that is given, is given for grasp, for mastery;
our hearts, lyric reeds in stormy, innate oceans.

On Online Dating

Ms. Volley-Chic, so glad you showed to chance
a Tuesday coffee date; I'm going to act
so fascinated with your brain and heart
before I cut and angle for your pants.

Ms. Sugardancer, really? Ready to date?
Please, try to hold out a bit longer.
That dampened, weaseled Kabuki theater
so commonplace, so not avant-garde.

Ms. Sexyone4u, your sudden, dramatic
revelation, your transformation from boy
back to girl, your attendant inner joy;
I shudder to contemplate your Socratic cave.

Ms. Good2no digs vulnerability
in *stronger* men? Guys, construct patinas
by reading Romantic poetry. Your feelings,
but rage and lust, may expand sensitively.

Ms. SoloBesaMe, what faint connection
pulls you toward another? You swore such tug
was creature chemistry, electromagnetic
rhapsody of sorts, not loss or horn.

Ms. Lovely4Surprise, girls be crazy!!!
Our candidly misaligned age may just
prevent boredom, add spice, inject lust.
I'm totally fit: firm dick, no hidden malaise.

Ms. AllTheBases, Meiji shogunates nixed
mixing among actor, artist, and prostitute.
But we *Love Suicides* email first or call a bit,
then eyeball-to-eyeball for lunch; acid test.

Ms. MerryOne, remark on Shackleton's
ad: *Men wanted for hazardous journey.*
Low wages, bitter cold, doubtful return.
Honour and recognition if survive successfully.

Pantoum: Meditation While Washing Laundry

If you do it with a feather, it's erotic.
If you do it with the whole chicken, it's perverted.

—Contemporary bumper sticker

Kenmore gloss-white washing machine, you idiot savant—
dgalosh ganosh dgalosh ganosh dgalosh ganosh.
To exorcize our dirt, we walk down stairs toward hell.
That darkness, past the water heater, behind the furnace. . . ?

Dgalosh ganosh dgalosh ganosh dgalosh ganosh.
Like automatic sex. Thoughtless killing. Helpless reflex.
In darkness—past the water heater, behind the furnace—
I gently crush and feel Donna's and Robyn's dirty beige panties.

Automatic sex. Thoughtless killing. Almost reflexively,
laundry falls into light, dark piles. De mundo here, de spirito there.
I gently crush and feel Donna's and Robyn's dirty beige panties;
I put each in my mouth and suck out their sweet, steely spots.

Man falls into light and dark piles—de mundo here, de spirito there.
Who is the thief but a person come to terms with ruthlessness?
I put each in my mouth and suck out their sweet, steely spots.
One is not ashamed of them, but still one apologizes.

Who is this thief? A person come to terms with ruthlessness,
who walks furtively down stairs toward hell—to exorcize dirt?
One is not ashamed of him, but still one is apologetic.
His skill and focus, like a detached machine—an idiot savant.

Trophy

Still in her freezer
after thirty years,
inside triple
Zip Lock bags,
a common carrot,
crevassed and shrunken.

At age thirteen
and five-eighths,
lying on the white
and pink squares
of a used kitchen floor,
used impatiently,
instrumentally,
to deflower.

To her recent
husband, cleaning the
refrigerator
Saturday morning:
Don't—
it has precedence.

Woman Marries Iguana, Carries Eggs

She liked his cold skin, the constant panting movement
    of vestigial gills.
At night next to him, she gave up fears just before sliding
    into formless dreams
of plains dotted closely by Acacia trees.

The morning of the first Tuesday of their second year
    she found a bundle of off-white
eggs under the couch at the end of a trail of slime.

After the third day, after he had been circling and circling
    the couch—first clockwise,
then counterclockwise, then clockwise again—
she brought out her dustpan to scoop up the wet
    stringy bundle

and lay it down underneath
    the warm gas stove.

To Lorna Doone from Her Husband, John, after Twenty Years of Marriage

Lorna Doone: A Romance of Exmoor

—R. D. Blackmore

Sweat just pinking your skin. An appearance
of lovely intelligence.
The throw of your head, black hair, back and up.
Oh, Lorna! This instant, love again.
In the carry of the line of all your bones
I see your charter—*Forward!* A stirrup
and a surly roan await their equestrienne.
Your look is simple, honest, full of spirit.
A spasm between my shoulders, my eyes flame.

I see our own
burly Western moors, our farm at Plover's Barrow.
I see us castling rook with king. There is infinite
here; someday that I will unknow.

Second Part: Death

Mud Dauber Wasp Nest

Monk at the Moment of Enlightenment
—Wood carving, Asian Art Museum, Seattle

That little yellow dauber wasp
worked and flew until it dropped.
Until the end of every blessed day
it flew straight, never lost its way.
Found the dirt, mixed the water,
hefted tiny gobs, daubed the mortar.
Never wondered if this mixture
might represent some wider picture—
some perfect mix of *form* and *function*.

Function—raise a progeny within asylum.
Form—daub a ball, a safer nest, a quiver.
Is this a bumbling wasp's ancient elixir,
or ordained by phylum's older nature?
Some Yung Dynasty's expert woodcarver
captured that monk's hot blaze of mystery.

But dauber wasps are *born* consistent—
born enlightened—carry water carry mud;
no need to prize a finger off far-off moons.
It knew well its place in time and space;
no need to plan on how to find a grace.

But then it found a perfect final resting bed—
a nest inside a monk's empty wooden head.
A leavened monk stares off beyond rare air;
but essences of tiny wasp beat him there.

In a Hostage Situation: A Play in Four Acts

Set:

The embassy's library. *The Economist*, June 12th, 1962, on a settee. Cover photograph—an old four-master putting out to sea at last. The thick, green, ceiling-high Bulgarian drapes are half-drawn over vertical, leaded windows.

Act 1:

Two circles, like picket fences, of scarf-and-necktie-bound arms. The bathroom door wedged fully open—by a *crack!* of an abductor's polished heel against a plastic wedge: *No, door open! No choice.*

Act 2:

Those trained beforehand, of course, keep eyes lowered, keep faces mild and mouths passive. But those untrained— their nostrils are too parched for snot or eyes for salt water.

Curtain and Intermission:
Chorus, in soft cadence, repeated until curtain rise:
   To not sing.
   To listen and wait.
   To listen and not sing.
   To not forget to beat your heart.

Act 3:

Bound men sitting in their circle act (or are) nihilistic. Bound women sitting in their circle act (or are) stoic. Children seem to act (or are) clear-minded and studious.

Act 4:

Faces take on a 'snowy' look (c.f. notes); some mouth a *Paternoster* when the attaché's punctured bullterrier tumbles out over the sill. *Go head on, Dude*, a pointed man shrills, not to anyone in particular, *Fear no evil!* He seems (or acts) to seethe within his still points.

38

Coda:

Chorus, in soft cadence, repeated until curtain:

To not sing.

To not ring bells.

Grasshopper, oh, grasshopper,

do not ring bells.

Male Sperm Counts Are Falling All Across the Western World

Around foreign towns, all mutts begin to bark
en masse. Seen beside a lazy, plumed lizard
asleep and hazy, sunning on a bare, flat rock
such musicality unsettles; and thus mirrors

qua Hermes' baleful caution: *Let's not relent!*
Scalped by psyche's past or divers ill fortune,
how decipher such a black-swan, wan event?
Populaces dimly heed *any* flood-tide moon;

apace, they *never* sort out or clear, clear text
from crypto. Even Diogenes fumbled vulgar acts;
will cosmic brains ever sift out scruffy pretexts?
Still, this seems to be an uncommanded rollback.

Green you, look deep at blunt-spoken metaphors;
mull Nature's murky nature; fret Loki's temblor.

After Chopping off Dozens of Mouses' Heads
Suddenly We Understood Literature

*The history of literature follows closely
the development of civilization.*

—Wikipedia

Alongside the cocked, spring-loaded mechanism's stainless blade, still-warm mice scurry aimlessly inside a small, plexiglass lab box, anxiously lapping water from feeding tubes. What do they smell?

Unlike Lakota war chief Crazy Horse at Little Big Horn, in the 1881 *Leavenworth Times*, and unlike Robert Jordan in *For Whom the Bell Tolls*—there in Segovia's pine-needles, bleeding to death—none of today's twenty-five mice squeaked, "This is a good day to die."

Unlike Arthur, conveyed via Morgaine's fairy barge to Avalon, those mice did not whisper, ". . . was it all for nothing then, what we did, and all that we tried to do?" The extant lumps, the quivering tails, are laid on a stainless tray and conveyed, respecting lab directives, to a mounting cremation pile.

Did those mice, like Jan Rodricks in *Childhood's End*, experience a profound sense of emptiness when all materiality instantly dissolved into white transparency? Did they feel no fear, only a powerful sense of fulfillment, as everything evaporated in a flash of light?

Dag Hammarskjöld's poignant 1952 entry in *Markings*: ". . . the hardest thing of all—to die rightly—an exam nobody is spared." Did they share those highfalutin' convictions?

None of tomorrow's twenty-five mice, like Carton in *A Tale of Two Cities*, will squeak, "It is a far, far better thing that I do, than I have ever done; it is a far, far better rest that I go to than I have ever known." Why save a Darnay from the Reign of Terror?

Unlike Countess Anna Arkadyevna Karenina—never so pure in that novel—tomorrow's mice will not volunteer death, underneath flying trains and clicking steel wheels, over jealousy and irrationality, confusion and anger.

But for them, a literary redemption: the lab's PI will publish a research article in *Nature* on the effects of L-ascorbic acid on overdosed mouse brains.

The Altar Fires

—W. S. Merwin, in memoriam

They sent the one who loves him best
to fetch him back to daphnied hell,
that hell that every maker sighs,
that peers of every stripe indwell.

There the Great Inscriber beams;
grasps the workman's hand, hands
him pen and ink and posts him off
to rosewood office workbench.

A sea of faces—some he knew:
    one who'd writ of marrow-bones
    one who'd writ of eyes and bees
    a third who'd writ of mouse's teats
    the last who'd writ of Aphrodite.

With that the man inspirits, begins
with forms and songs to lay his art
to blaze the path for those, like I,
who follow far, so far, behind.

Fatherland

A man dies and is buried. He is a family man, a father.
His wife and children lie stripped of all purpose, can
never look up at light again until their lives unscramble,
then perhaps may be able to eat a full balanced meal.

A man dies and is buried. He is mirror, is counter cycle.
He is Jew, is Ichthyosaurus, is swamp. Left school at age 12.
Comes in time to be the last man alive on a dying Earth.
Guards his brood as animal wife swims out to hunt herring.

A family man, a father, dies, is buried. Is *Love Supreme,*
is love for muse, is faith, is love for God. Rises to jazz bardo.
Like Jim Thompson, in 39th year is stalked by leopard, eaten.
Wife—*Hurrah!* Goes to spit on his abusive, alcoholic gravesite.

A man dies. He knows many things; teaches sewing or carburetion
to daughters who find wives to make sons who in turn, father sons.
A husband loves his wife deeply but never understands what is love.
A man dies, will get up next morning to go work to feed his family.

A man dies and is not buried, but his heart is still warm, so Crazy
Horse and his warriors cut it out of him and eat it, still warm.
A man dies; his wife teaches singing at Yale while he goes to hunt
the Serengeti; he scales acacias at night to sleep, to avoid leopards.

A man is overcome, dies in scrambled purposes. Is a common man.
A man enjoys fat women with curly hair. He is the last happy father.
A man is Siddhartha's father. Is Don Juan in Hell, kicks Devil's ass.
A man, Siddhartha, dies and is buried. He is family man, a father.

Circling on the Edge of the War Zone

Tonight I stand the third sonar watch alone,
self-contained. Eyes are useless here;
best forgotten or lightly closed. Light
is what I hear and shadow, the time between
whines and cries above of mating right whales.

Our all-black, unnumbered boat floats at great depth.
Tonight nothing in this South China Sea
is quieter. Like a great, black, tethered planet
its steel hull drifts in monotonous circles, grazing
the War Zone's eastern edge. A clock's caged face
reads 1903 Zulu. Tomorrow we start back for Papa Hotel.

In dense, black sea above, I imagine
two whales flying a reckless Immelmann maneuver.
At the top of their long, arching curve
they join themselves and fall back towards me.
But I do not hear their cries now; like me, they listen.

I imagine that three hundred miles to the west,
perhaps even to Laos, dozens of all-black B-
52s begin their flawless nightly bombing run.

Dirty Dead Prick Fish

Salutations, um? So down-and-out, you're sure to bless the sky for no rain. Go scatter incense sticks around your baseness; they will not be of service; you've gone too far. All hollow inside—no liver, guts, nor medial prostate; your so-called brain down to a thin gauze stem, then redacted into elevated dis-timelessness, into some far-behind country. The earth-moles won't look you in the eye and vultures just shit on you.

We'll find a big iron vise, you dirty dead prick fish, and make you small, tiny; slide you down a kitchen sink drain, into p-traps to under-sea cloacas, downstream to the local treatment plant; you'll be aerated in some fetid holding pool to a far-forward time and place—so, no redemption, you.

Eat that recompense, you dirty dead prick fish. You have no short future in any known universe. We shall dissect your foul attitudes, push them down, deep down, into a clay Begonia flowerpot. If we ever glance at you again, what's better than to not roam back into happiness and bright lights.

You will be amazed, honey, she said, at the end, at the importance of Berloiz's soft cello on your useless, furtive brain. Remember, you are either a victim or a volunteer, so when that fuzzy cloud dims a light, the chill returns. Eclipsed is for the better

Strait of Georgia

A modern fairy-tale, in such a pelagic time of essence?
What happened, amid three plates, to raise a rebellion?
Rebellion used to mean, to throw a sabot into gears;
this fairy-tale's hot undercarriage throws up—cornelian.

A black-flagged schooner goes down in a flash storm.
Strait of Georgia, Salish Sea, Texada Is., Fraser River:
their undercrusts, disturbed, contrive a wet, top bomb.
Waves, waves, waves swamp a homeport latecomer.

But Strait of Georgia will love this happy sailor; his
ascension sends him up, contented, to bless a wavy
air-rind, to boil breath back to starved lungs, to fuse
at once his depth-misted, near-field, watery ennui.

All declinations of bluefish and blue fish, sea floors,
sea fans tilt to face the Sea of Trees by eternal Mt. Fuji.
Echoes slosh, tidy at first, then raise up wave-doors.
Capitulate thee now, sense an utter oncoming beauty.

After a Train There'd Be a Fit

Gone halfway up the hill above railroad tracks
to take the free-swinging rope in both my hands
and lean back, thinking hard, how, many years past,
I would have glared down that slab of sand—

steep, crossed, and crimpled with live-oak roots,
ended below by a wide, green-plagued ditch—
then lifted up my happy feet to plunge far out,
spun around, strained against an outward pitch,

shrieking, laughing, a mild, soaring lark.
But now I tie that knotted swing-rope back
across a zinc spike angled through rough bark.
I stare down that foreign, tilted, sandy bank

to see my thoughtless body splash that fetid quag.
I can precisely name each worn-bare root I'd hit;
at end, my body'd slam halfway across the track.
After a train there'd be a fit.

Were We Really So Happy Back Then?

We still carry on as we did back then,
but aren't we now quite so wistful?
Such conceit—climb down, blind sister!
Now decades pass; that fanciful old ken,
if so sweetly wonderful, why hadn't we
deployed it to emasculate seedy bourgeoisie?

No, tomorrow will never become today,
nor will last year again misrepresent itself,
nor appear as if to turn over some new leaf,
nor concoct any rare, eternal half-delay.
Is that decades-old bloom off today's rose?
(Low tropic sun circles my subzero snow.)

Calico cat, doggerel dog, sad parakeet;
lobster and conch my evening supper;
houseboy, yardboy, laundress (all colored).
Never need money; our class—upper elite.
Barred windows; brother's top bunk bed.
Dad shot my lovely old Peggy in the head.

The Literal Mind Was Crushed

After seven days of round-the-clock jackhammers
and hot-tempered chisels, the bones surrendered.

The hands, which were to be sent to watchmakers,
kicked up, incessantly pantomiming.

The feet were toenailed onto sunflower
stems; both sent, heads bowed, captive, to Diaghilev.

Since there was so little heart there to speak of,
the cavity stored C-clamps and wisps overnight.

The brain auditioned but was deemed of slight use
except to tare scales—and there it failed,
since whatever it thought of, it contracted.

The literal mind was crushed to end idolatry.

At the end, only the soul remained intact,
glistening in a pool of body fluids.

Meditation on a Trash Fire in My Backyard

There was a type of black there that invited
roughing. The fire was the first element,
a type of mist coming out of baked
earth. There, I could tear off my shoes, leap
at once to the center of coral-white coals.
Of pyre-building and self-immolation, nothing's
obvious; they are fashionable graces.

Which I did over and over one winter
there at Chincoteague Island. I leased an antique
cabin—clapboard, no insulation—
an old Vogelzang stove for cooking, heat.
Occasionally I left the grated door ajar
to illuminate any sudden, basal nature of flame.

    Ponies, conditioned for ages, sense heat and smoke.
    They push their dark, curvaceous noses up against
    a leeward thin-glass window; tip over a
    tenant's sympathy, get an apple, a scrap, a mango.

Would you have taken my hand in yours, joined me on that
pyre, suffered unctuous pains, helped us across
the gulf into a pureland? At that penultimate
second, I would do it for you dear—I would
always turn back to look for you, sweet.

    Left-over that late evening: your ring, my ring—
    gems upon a burned earth—then, a month or two,
    a pink crystal tree germinates, full-
    grown. That art—to reach there, pick off a sliver
    of glass, take it home, worship it.

And Pity Those Who Lost Their Grip

Were gravity the other way
perhaps the strangeness that we felt
would come to mean as little or less
than upside-downness does today.

Were gravity the other way
we'd admire roots instead of flowers,
hang for hours out from bowers,
watch the bees buzz 'round and play.

Were gravity the other way
Rapunzel with her golden hair
would drop it up the farthest tower,
save her knight from a lonely stay.

And pity those who lost their grip
were gravity the other way.

On the Earth of Lincoln County, Washington, on Saint Valentine's Day, 1993

February 14, observed in honor of St. Valentine,
a martyr of the third century, beheaded in Rome.

—Wikipedia

Dismemberment of a junked disk harrow
proceeds evenly and eventlessly.
The earth of Lincoln County petitions
lithe, dank, midmorning fog to settle low.

The fog is dense and, like a just-washed shroud,
droops to raw ground between dull, browned edges
of cold iron. On this Valentine's Day,
Lincoln County martyrs a threadbare plow.

Disk harrows, plows, reaping machines, combines—
each led, as its time comes, to a high spit
of farmland among wild blackberry vines
and nine discarded mounds of field-turned stones

and left. First in, next spring: blackberry shoots,
their sap charged with Lincoln County's thawing
sod. Thorns find and rack the combine's core; wedged
ice severs a nameplate from a chaff chute:

```
+——————————————————————————+
| Wayne and Son Farm Implement Company   |
| St. Cloud, Minnesota              1950 |
| Patent No.                      97,802 |
+——————————————————————————+
```

After forty Junes, red thorns gird debris

mounded and fertile as plow-horses' dung.
Iron disks, forged during this passion play's
acts, are shards by the last. Medea's outdone.
Earth is a cannibal eating her young.

Along the Shore

—Mimi Baez Fariña, in memoriam

Winds out of the SSE form and preserve high ocean curls
and along a changed shore, life lives or dies in tiny increments;
put your ear down now into that wet, shifting sand.

What's the music bled out of that high-crashing surf?
If you listen very closely, what you may hear
is a rising and falling harmony of slush and simile.

At what point did your entire universe shift to desert,
dry and lifeless, shift back to adversity, seem annexed?

When in spite of crushing forces laid upon you, when
at last you were just given to sing, you survived

powerfully. In time, your song shifted into feeling
and at that point you climbed up to higher, fitted peaks

to look out over a fertile valley, over some flat tabletop.
Now break out of your tunnel, find lasting calm in honor.

And what's divine out of all this, this mess?
Only the kiss of your wave's moving curl

as you glide along, as your native blackbird
batters at walls of a too-stringent tunnel.

What a long deluge of light—so push down then,
down harder on your ancient reverberator pedal.

Winds blow back to her, blow
her strengthening self back at us.

Death Is Pique

And we are so vexed because,
well, which door *do* we go through?
Empty is how this leaves us feeling.

It's like a fey lifeboat: all around
us, but taking on water
faster than we can toss it out.

So, bail faster or tread water—or,
now bereft, we could surely castle,
feint, free our life-blood to rook.

Eridanus, Mythical River

I. The overture

Gifted hunter—please stay, listen, Eridanus murmured. *I have much to teach you.*
I was puzzled, paused. This overture—teach me what, and why? And, at what price?
Ah, you've paid already, the river rustled. *What, you don't yet know.*

I drew back. Who trafficked here first—Hephaestus? *He* was lame.
  Did he . . . him too?
Man always denies the wrong thing, scolded the water. *Such a frail device.*
Hephaestus? Fa! Consider—feel my truth. I swear, I do have much to teach you.

I knew my mind itself to be a hunter's greatest enemy. Now mine was like snow.
What price, I wondered? *This river—it's dark as ink,* I snorted. This is *radiance?*
Water gnawed the bank, spat: *You've paid, gifted hunter; what, you don't yet know.*

Just then, a strong wind overworked the river's surface. Even if, if long ago,
I *had* paid, I did know my mind. I leaned forward. *Is there another way . . . a place?*
The reach was blunt: *Strike your bargain, man; I've little time—much to teach you.*

What incredible, what cold wind! Now I felt so aidless (was I?) and bent so low.
Had I known what word, what genius, the river sought; had my life been
  more chaste.
Eridanus strained: *Come—what you don't know, so never thought, won't hurt you.*

II. The cadence

We do what we can, and there is much importance to starting right. Plow
a twisted row if you must—better that than an unturned field. *Your true*
cost? A fruitless abstraction. Never mind, I have much to teach you,
Eridanus muttered. *You've paid already; what price, you will soon know.*

Assemblage: On a South Dakota Chain Gang in Autumn, 1958—Air, Ants, and Fervid Thinking

Late afternoon, with Big Evans as third of eight.
When his bowels made a sharp after-lunch noise,
in mid-stride all five lagging convicts broke gait

to clear his pocket of welded air. I yanked loose
zinc-steel chains between my ankles taut—
I'd tied a loop of twine mid-links and noosed

it into the crook of my left arm. *Now*, I thought,
both hands are free for trash pickup. Then,
ten paces out and left, Lucidor raised his .30-06

(it had the 'scope for long-range work; the close-up,
finish bit was Kevin's; he carried the sawed-off)
to smoothly mock a shot at Evans, cross hairs lined up

on the lime bull's-eye stenciled onto his brown
jumper just below shoulder blade and left of spine.
On the next step all five came back into line, bent down

to study green moss doing cabotage in ragged lines
along crevasses in the blacktop's edge. Just behind, I
heard tinkling—Kevin sipping from the guard's IcyFine?

I'd filled their cooler at dawn; its dewy side stamped *Guards
Use Only.* I focused, blinked. A mass of ants swarmed
across the blacktop, moss, and gravel underfoot—thousands,

in random, tumbled order—a dull, black velvet minuet
churning out of three ocherous anthills. T. H. White's
vision—Arthur metamorphosed into an ant—and Merlin's tenet

—*Everything Not Forbidden Is Compulsory*—both instantly abided.
Then, over my north shoulder, a noisy flock of—willets? couldn't
look—winged toward the Gulf; a long-range, winter *Les Sylphides.*

58

My Transuranium Goblet

—For A. Q. (Abdul Qadeer) Khan

He blusters, *Happy exaltations! The bomb is ours;*
never again suffer such humiliations. Two
fingers at the anti-Muslim West—*Up yours!*

Used fortune-tellers to time detonations, but so loved—
Pakistan my country, it was dismembered!—animals,
built a pet sanctuary to sequester stray birds and dogs.

Sold bomb innards. *Above laws! Not a nut or mad-mind!*—
Made Pakistan integral—*But yes, a demigod to my people*—
to the Muslim world. Clever, covert, so clandestine,

spun-up a half-million Muslim centrifuges worldwide.
While under house arrest, he pirated from North Korea,
set up nuclear black markets for uranium hexafluoride.

Convicted then pardoned by Musharraf—too late:
Hindus and Christians had it; why not my Muslims?
Who made the Muslim bomb? Only me—I made it!

The trick is told when the trick is sold.

Kids Just Getting off the Ferry

A vast chorus of happy chatter as their ferry slides in
Pillows underarm, they come from a weekend retreat
They have tickets as long as summer in tattered rear
pockets
Their floating ribs are arcs sailing into blondness and
straight A's, poppies and bubblegum
Every one of them cut on a bias, a lotus in mud
Joking, poking one another, high spirits, they shag,
shuffle along the dock, so unschooled *in extremis*
Columns of puppy smells going up and up
See lemonade everywhere, endless lemonade
Wildness in their young furies
Always another weekend, always another passionate
Cars and kissing and fumbling with buttons and catches
Toss a charm in the air, each of them catches it behind
their back
They think they have no body, just cotton candy
Foreign suns blaze eternally down their necks
They will entangle their legs at ankles endlessly,
instantly
Girl or boy angels dance on their burgeoning
shoulders—fragile umbrellas to ward off
Raw fingerlings, each coasting into limitlessness; so
like triangles—all sides the same
Unfixed as ocean water; captured in pale amber, they
carry no dirt undersole; love is in their air
Lifeguards muse of boys and love, sweet after-hours
sex
Knowledge of determinate evil yet to manifest
Angels grow old and die but time to leave earth—not
ever
How can they not think of themselves so much?
Forever onward, sunlight will be on their brittle torsos
Tomorrow will still find ferries waiting to board them

THIRD PART: Literature

Pressure Changes at Snow Lines
—After Louis MacNeice's "Snow"

Dreaming, we wake upon our dream to hear
upon a stand of pale horses, happy
in their element, and free, and feel
their manes swinging way, and back. Across
their arced necks a lively floss of snow

stains their dark. Their dreams will float down,
encompassed not by willingness, but by
frosts that pack the underearth until
a thaw can throw them back at oxygen.

Our dreams lilt like certain fire on snow
lines playing horses have packed; they snort
and paw and flirt and nip, mount vermillion
dreams up on their backs, race them off
at snowy rivulets, at sinks of cold.

Now warm and windy weather sends
crepuscular dreams to fleet among
a mane; every green leaf that buds
in March discloses its line of snow
as feelings condense. But hints of young

planets puzzle theorists, because
god is everywhere, is everything.
So how might his work not be done
that seventh day of far-out snow lines—
the distance from a star beyond our souls.

A Bee in Late October

Abuzz on tarmac, a-verve in honey quest
we lift and toss a bumblebee to grass.
Why there, why now; why long apart its harness?
Bee, capitulate to winter, prepare your nest!

But did we do enough or do much less?
Afraid of sting, ingloriously shirked,
temperamental, well-unwise—we consigned
a fuzzy-thinking late-harvest bee

to forebear the cold, the ant, the sopping rain.
Oh, mourn not one simple bee. Like grains of sand
they subdivide. But what solipsists contend
is *flawed*—we and bee do abet; we enchain

the myth that babes whose lips are kissed by bees
become our sacred future poets, our seers.

A Young Flemish Scientist in Early Contemplation of Gravity and Light

—After *Young Woman with a Water Pitcher* by Johannes Vermeer

. . . I saw it yesterday again—again.
Aloft, mending a transept split by winter ice,
the steeplejack's felt hood blew clean away.
I counted and paced; two, then three, next four.
On five, it skimmed a puddle of melt.
My count and pace were five; the same, exact
same, count of five a shattered brick felled
to earth, to God; the pastor's cow last May
when sun unglued that frozen eastern cornice.
What drew my heeding, my father's inward gulp.

. . . five then; five now. So, were I to fling
this pitcher down, would cream and brass—how odd—
alight at once? My maid could count. No, better I. . . .
My father, bless him, disagrees. Says we counted faster;
nay, counted wrong. But did my heart not beat
to keep that pace? Small matter!

. . . ah, precious, this chiseled window's beveled edge,
admitting red and blue and royal purple tints.
Just an instant's touch, a breath, amends this patent fan.
But whence? The sun's but yellow. The sky, but blue.
My headdress, white. The table's rug, red. That steady fire,
our sun, so piques my curiousness. A furled anagram?

. . . well, this Spring, our windowmaker's back.
I'll ask, delicately, would he craft for me
a private bar of clearest glass and sharpest bevel?
For a few guilders? Father, perhaps. . . .

. . . again, that shattered brick. Again, I see its arc
from cornice down to cow. I chart its flight.
Ah, that tinted fan of light—Lord, those selfsame arcs. . . .

Hive

Tall building,
insolent hive,
rich with money,
swarming with drones—
your Queen is dead!

Who will be the one
to lay you in her hand
and now, like Excalibur,
draw you forth
from the blind earth?

The Orb Weaver

Blind prey-insect blunders into *Araneida*'s
sticky weblines. The orb weaver scuttles
out to sting and stun, then wrap in silk,
a late-night gift-snack.

The prey's orb-path, a path of no-return, no followings-on.
Occasionally scuttling out for my own little followings-on,
whom do I meet coming in on the way back? Myself,
or a pettier self, or even a flock of iridescent starlings
en masse looping around, reversing course and flying
backwards to some simpler time—perhaps 1895—
to a strange contraption enwrapped by two crosswise,
double-orbed loops. Day and night flapping around
faster and faster until, at end, George, the English scientist
and his device, slow to alight in A.D. 802,701, to find
an invisible Oort Cloud surrounding Weena, us, and him;
Earth, asteroids, everything we love or hate, pray to, kill for.

Underneath all, an unseen, illusory ring of fire encircles
light-fearing Morlocks and Pacific Rim alike; constrains
the sundry lithospheric orbits of hot, young,
tectonic plates. Come over to the edge, take a look.

Well, there is no edge; no edge to navigate me through
my weaknesses, get me around my awkward sentimentalities.
What needs observing is my careless—in all minutiae—
vanishing point of true purpose.

Like that old-time projector—all gears, reels, clamps,
and pulleys—that streamed 1946's *The Catman of Paris*
and scared the living hell out of a young boy who,
on the fly, had to learn to splice snapped celluloid loops
with a sharp bias cutter and bicycle glue. A sad dis-learning
orbit: courting, marriage, divorce, then courting
again—bloody circularities. Once I played coy;

now I concede: North Atlantic Deep Water will recycle
its dense, cold, salty northern seas down and across
to the warm Gulf Stream.

Everything changes, everything is connected: a duo-dharma cycle.
Electrons, darning needles, period punctuation marks, moon
cycles, palindromes, weird topologies—as when a Poincaré
3-sphere turns inside out—what's left over? Deep endlessness:
Klein bottles, Möibus strips, Escher stairways, buttocks,
my own stunned, conceited, backlands moulderings.

A Compass Only Spins That Finds No Source
—Sonnet for three voices

Muse:
My tongue is dumb, like a bee long past autumn.
I guide the shuttle but never weave the tapestry.
I forge all names: rat, and color of chrysanthemum.
Among a modest tribe of sisters, I call no country
home but heart. So this, my only lee:
to gerrymander all her tics and blocks
since when a writer writes she speaks for me.
Her playful hand my silent maze unlocks.

Poetess:
A medlied stream, I'm fixed to run amok
and breech these Christless banks that vise my course.
But etch an outlying field or splinter rock?
A compass only spins that finds no source.

Witness:
Hermetic rule or perfectly affable law?
What slim equilibrium between need and awe.

The Pale Wall Became the Mind Itself

> After "The House Was Quiet and The World Was Calm"
> —W. Stevens

The pale wall standing in front of him was a lake.
Then, in his mind, the pale wall became the mind itself

and the pale now-mind imagined it was falling into
a windowless room. The surface of the falling

lake was nearly flat; as it fell toward him, he leaned
slowly into its conscious surface and looked beneath.

He saw his thoughts there like white salamanders.
The wall shimmered with all the thoughts underneath.

But the lake was flat still and, running into its deepest
parts, the thoughts left no lasting trace of their passing.

Then the pale lake's water itself became one sole
thought and, with mind and wall, came close to rest.

Rue, Herb of Grace

Take care when grasping rue, the herb of grace;
it coaxes absent periods, heals the heart,
and kills—if hills, an old wall, do not balance.

To nix, sprinkle holy water; but first, slash rue's bark.

Oh, witches, scorpions, orders of black art,
heed Mithridates, King of Pontus, Greece:
*Pick five fresh leaves of rue; add salt, impart
a fig, beat and drink—then clap for Circe.*

Rue thrives best if stolen first, but then released.

First strip stems, then fuse—an ancient, Christless rune:
*Twelve bitter, atonic leaves in piss shocks priests
to second sight; three more, they'd marry the moon.*

Bay gifts honor, and lavender, acceptance;
but glandy, blue-leaved, bitter rue—repentance.

Year of the Gnat

A string of twelve moons across a crisp horizon;
gnats too dance at night, not resting nor sleeping,
they drink up the moon's light in sips, in sips.
Slack time for them is now; they converse,
make plans, compare dress;
small, but attuned to the pull of moon gravity.

Outside, a dizzy scene upends and regroups
through two hundred pairs of so-ended eyes
wiped clean by winglets sparkling in faint light;
if they come out again to an early next sun, they are blinded.
Two or three hundred swarm, not alighting—tornadoes
dancing on silent air. This must be their time to rise up to me
    —but so futile.

Then shall I use them to float up, to fly up to my own swarm?
Their wisdom is of their soul.
Their sunlight expands my blood.
But I do not understand any of this: what I have done,
what I will do, and it matters not
if I see or do not see.

At the Greek temple of Delphi, at the navel of Gaia,
I stood and looked down, far into the valley of Phocis below.
I, always a constant linear, felt of Delphi's relentless vortexes.
This is the temple of Apollo, Apollo's sacred precinct;
rise up gnats, you are efflux—of the god of sun and light, of his soul—
you are in the float.

The Cow that Makes Cream

After "The Emperor of Ice-Cream"
—W. Stevens

Call the artificial inseminator,
the long-armed vet, and chance him thrust
into her livid womb waggling worms.
Make the stable hands clean up the mess
as they are used to buffalo chips. Let girls
cool her fervor with languorous songs.
Let bees be flattened on screen.
The only cow is the cow that makes cream.

Take the three-legged stool that stoops,
lacks balance, and squeaks, has nicks
where she broke clean my left leg once.
Place it close alongside her udders.
If my hands are cold or damp, they serve
to less misdirect the flow and not swerve.
Let the milk commence its gleam.
The only cow is the cow that makes cream.

A Puzzle on the Table inside M.V. *Chetzemoka* Underway

A flat cow, half *sur le table*,
attenuating in the hot summer
air, moos silent discontent—
her midsection's soft jagged ends
inquire after her missing remainder.

A blood-red barn, sliced open, breaks
in waves right across a hayloft door;
other half down on the upper deck,
brushed by some rushing passenger.
Half-on, half-off—no piton to hook onto.

Off a dim, half-visible corner, astride an
old Chiron, a jagged man lays requisite
tolls in a pilot-master's upheld palm:
Well, you shouldn't *understand until
our ferry kisses that far-over shore.*

That puzzle—pray it ends amply for all:
for cow, half-horse, barn, ferry-master,
and man. Five pieces left to go;
fit them in and then go file ashore?

Or, pitch them over port-side rail to naked
water, reverse course, back to breath?

Final Canticle, on the Tools for Cultivation
of Our Own Secret Garden

Without having to think exactly, our consensual hearts (colored like Adonis's petals) know that the right tool for tilling lies somewhere beneath the frost-buckled crust, just in front of a long pile of broken obelisks.

This right tool will carve out rot, plaster up rabbit-gnawed carrots, reverse ears of corn inside husks, talk to lawn spiders, geyser aerated water every thirty-two minutes, have a pink-plateaued handle, loll around the corner of the tool shed between uses, smell like my girlfriend's arm on early weekend mornings, shoot electric bolts of horse energy into the dirt, clear a path through a closed winter garden like a Soviet icebreaker, between plunges into the earth enlist nematodes for a metal concert, and will not ever be disfranchised.

Below the Technicolor roots of this garden—exactly what *is* happening?—the humus is twisted in inordinate complexity, isomorphic to dust clouds in the Horsehead Nebula. Even darker human sources in an upstairs garden apartment contemplate a complete massacre of the squashes. Here and there are pictographs of beets starved by the domination of the ash tree.

A desperate charisma reigns. It attaches to the spade, the hoe, the quailing hand-plow. But when we dig in, the garden's heat alchemizes us, and so we become *transeunt.*

π Covered in Whipped Cream

Come on, this is just us having some insider fun
about mathematics (which *will* be annotated).

To begin, we saw the sous-chef chuck the cream
on thick. And ever since then, what? Manifestly

sticky, π-able, fallen nutcakes! Rifle well-regarded,
obscurant journals all the way back to Ur-Babylon

for best recipes; you may wander far, even to null
green-fields, to search or even to certify an absolute.

If necessary, you might take a friendly date with
three fellows: Emerson, Euler, and Gamma,

a brightest set of serious transcendentalists, who
all buy tickets to this day's minor-league game,

slosh hot dogs with mild Dijon, argue in loud, bounded,
gutter Italian about warm butterscotches, *quozientes,*

or even the *inherent goodness of nature.* Bypass a shaky
proof; skirt an irrational, hard-to-master lemma; best

course is stick to facts. If the third, fifth, or eighth inning
is boredom, play the thirteen-question game: pick some

never-ending name, π is a good one to start with.
Well, so much depends upon the buckled twist

of its surrounding ground—flat, Gaussian, saddle-backed,
or back-bucked—lays that render it tremulous, shaky, or open.

Even manifolds with endless digits will not do justice,
so, golly, truncate. Perhaps it's a time and place to pick

a ripe Sagittarian to go and order at the unbounded
concessionaires: *Three icy-black supernova creams please,*

liberally sprinkled with Vegas on top, wholly girly strings,
and pink-dotted Cygnuses. Oh, truth and beauty, be

Gedanken-like, unite a few fuzzy horizons—wheel
and lark us on bright, axisymmetric, unphysical radii.

Symmetry

—Hermann Weyl, Princeton University Press, 1952, 168 pages

I.
Symmetry is only of the mind.
What—limitations?
Gedanken!

II.
Symmetry implies *axis.*
Axis implies *straight line.*
There are no straight lines.
Pale blue, maybe?

III.
Pulling g's like hell,
Thirty rev's a second—
where's up or down?
Feels like I'm in some
fricking dryer.
Next, I'll want to fly
an inside Immelmann.

IV.
Original sin transgresses:
the wafers, the wine
start flying around,
up and down.
If sin's so bad, can't we just please
go back to
plain old
sacrilegious lust?

V.

Dr. Hermann Klaus Hugo Weyl

addresses his Institute for Advanced Study's audience:

The operations of the group

consist of all possible rotations. . . .

He himself is abject circularity.

His blood moves from left to right,

from up to back down,

for just another three years.

VI.

Symmetry—such an odd creature!

If you turn it inside out,

turn it upside down,

mirror it left against right,

even pull it right back through itself,

it still behaves

like a silly old cat.

VII.

Of course, I'm a racist,

remonstrated the sparkling-bright sphere.

Who would want

their chosen son,

their chosen daughter,

to grow up, live their life,

in some queer topology

near-dominated

with a Spiral Jetty,

a Leaf Horn,

or a Broken Obelisk?

VIII.
The astonishing chambered
nautilus, Nautilus pompilius!
A continuous logarithmic
spiral, an infinite series of
chambers!
    Too bad.
Wrecked is the ship of pearl! / From
thy dead lips a clearer note is born. . .

IX.
The ensuing discussion
in the French Academy
was summed up by Fontenelle as Secrétaire perpétual
in a famous judgement
in which he denied
to the bees
the geometric intelligence of a Newton and Leibniz
but concluded that in using the highest mathematics
they obeyed divine guidance and command.

X.
Imagine our solar system
without shapefullness;
no regularity nor conventional *res.*
Imagine our beloved sun transformed
to a way-wicked cube
or a tossed-off heptahedron.
But we humans, we're
infinitely adaptable;
maybe in time we'd
get used to it.
Days would be stellar.

XI.
Weyl's time-honored symmetries—all
so universally secular.
Why? Maybe God our
Mandator in His early years
was a rebellious teenager.
Maybe had a distant, cold, blue-collar father.
Maybe all along He's really
just a silly old tomcat.

XII.
. . . we are about to turn
from art to nature. . . first consider
what one may call
the mathematical philosophy
of left and right. To the scientific mind
there is no inner difference,
no polarity between left and right,
as there is for instance
in the contrast of male and female. . . .

XIII.
There certainly must be
a Higher Plane of symmetry:
there, everything is Platonic;
there, Weyl is its handmaiden,
as are Gauss, Hilbert,
Poincaré.
And in time, that crazy Russian guy
Perelman, who in 2002 solved
Poincaré's Conjecture.
And Albert,
their highest nature.

XIV.
Play the hand you were dealt,
the wise, old academician
counsels to
the paraplegic
who, like Hawking,
carefully nudges
his round, rubber-coated wheels
backwards and forwards
an inch
then another.

XV.
The juncos up in
my flowering
quince chirp
and chirp
and chirp.
Their verbs billow out
across 360 degrees.
I meditate underneath, cross-legged
on my brown earth.
Above me,
drab females size up.

XVI.
A woman, 27-ish,
attractive,
complains
of condoms:
I hate cheap store-bought
kinds, the way
they are so squishy in use.
Thinking fast, I offer
to lend her ultrathin samples

from my back closet's upper shelf—
tubular-like but ancient, their atom-thinness
just now disintegrating.

XVII.
Architecture of a human brain:
. . . distributed along four functional axes:
symbolic communication, perception/action,
emotion,
and decision-making.
. . . male brains more asymmetrically
lateralized than those
of females.

XVIII.
A yellow-furred,
black-bodied
caterpillar crawls
across the tarmac
off to the northwest
to its end.
I stop a morning jog to look down.
Its slow, awkward
symmetries play
onto endless cycles.

XIX.
Long poems so dreadful?
Invoke symmetry!
Fold them up
along their edges,
make scintillating
origami
out of every
trailing stanza.

FOURTH PART: **Everything Else**

White, Black

Everything rests on the fine tip of intention,
said Grace. Her soft Buddhist dictum
was crystal-clear: only *two* paths to wisdom!

White path, a signal for upside penchant:
   Winter coat tossed to a hapless guy,
   donor buys another that same night.

Black motive concedes donor's conceit:
   One-up'd that poor sot!—most awry.

Hallelujah, empty out
both dresser drawers, go lay in laurels;
their wind exposes—their ancient wind opposes.

What flees apart thus founders; lends room
to all muddled, shaded truths. White plays
the lyre; redacted black reveals all misfalls.

Flash of Beauty

There was just a flash of beauty in my heart;
nothing cheap there, just the end of the line.

Evening barn swallows catapult, cartwheel,
dive; for them, what is near to beauty?
Acrobatic and so near to Zion, so near
to hidden Utopias—and their ancestors too
flashed above us all, like these present days.

What does, for an inscrutably consummate
mind, flash by—is what flashes by
like some half-twisting rainbow? Or perhaps
is a rare recipe for shivering dog-happiness?

Once upon a time, a million million years
ago, the bastard sky fled to fill a vast imagining.
Tantalus or his brother threw their dies far
out, and stumbled apace un-wholeheartedly

into old-Havana-like, golden terrariums
they would resurrect for the remainder
of their sequined lives.

Know you, the slow-dying earth cares nothing
for fixed lives, for great-beating hearts; be certain—
passing beauty will not be encircled nor ever bound.

House of Lords, Temporal and Spiritual

A long time ago
the sky fell.
A cloud caught the sky,
spun silver threads,
whistles, and songs.

If what happened was happy
then no more could be sung.
Peace over all the water column—
each one of you shall drink the water;
each one of you shall repeat the song.

Great heroes come and then leave;
such is the temporal.

A single bird dropped down into hell,
but it was enough
for fortune.

Again and again, clouds entrain:
No, never!

So, have you heard?
Loss makes everything safer.
The water becomes steadily cooler.
The Lords have made their bones.

Invasive Species

i.

My last, best, unstraight-laced ditchdigger
carried consternation over Jesus, LSD, and
Robert Lowell off to Nepal; there, she
painted Gods all in human skins, advised
dialogue over plot, and got shaped by tragedy.
She painted mornings' mountains out so far,

ii.

her dreams no longer felt their legerdemain.
A thousand winds blew through her each night.
She elbowed out a tiny niche, dug deep latrines,
dug deeper wells, their bottoms nearly mica mines.
At twenty-three, Pearl tampons ferried by monthly air.
No lovers; village elders nixed comingled strains.

iii.

She strides within her iridescent bubble, gazing over
sloping tides of scree—slick, glossy, treacherous, and
fetishized. Scarves, scarves twirl about her hot neck,
scattering tiny, alien passengers across the discotheque.
Barring grace, her *Be equals?* curtsy might be querulous;
her *I want to dance to your rock-'n'-roll* clashes with *Sarowar*.

iv.

Early on, she'd anticipated some spring—sure, or bounce—
but not this quixotic, subtle or not, tug-of-war
as in-country rectors civilly unsoftened their edges.
Wasn't it the *Age of Exploration*, she'd alleged?
Wasn't there some jointly happy shore? She thought
she'd ordered vichyssoise—instead got borscht.

Curious George and the Man with the Yellow Hat

The Man
With the Yellow Hat
Went deep
Into the forest wild
And brought out
An ever-curious
Primate
Who found
Everything in life
Hilarious and fresh.

Just like Zen eyes
And such.
Just like Beginner's Mind
And such.
Not exclusive to Human—
Also in Monkey Mind.

As Dr. Einstein once surmised,
The most important decision
An ever-curious monkey can make
Is whether his universe
Is a friendly place
Or that his universe
Is an unfriendly place—
Hostile or benign.

Inventing a New Color

In laze and spun together
we instantiate our colors
against the fall of night.

We see with critic's eyes
at first, and gull too much
to soften each soft hand;

then smear a grainy gesso
to constrict our *pentimenti*
to indelible intents.

But imprinted in our frame
is evidence of leanings
on why to square a circle.

In time our brush unveils
a swerving of the heart
that goads, at last, élan.

The Empty Quarter
—The Rub' al Khali

This empty quarter inside him,
inside his still-beating heart,
was full of song and fun.
There was loud pizzicato music
and air and spirits flying about
all bright things in sight.

Maybe there shouldn't have been:
dry sands looked fine all alone,
the souls of earth flying in and out
of hands of prose and feelings.
His sun had long since emptied out,
been filled with silica, with myrrh.

Rahsaan Roland Kirk's sax song
drives up into dry, sad earth, makes
it fertile for play, for after life—
for *vivezza* and vibrancy, much
openness and joyfulness, as if
his skies arced fully up to apogee.

Tear the dunes away, back into
empty centers of language of air;
Rahsaan's music hits its up-marks,
weaves just above hot quartz. Lost
here and there, and all around, are
doors, but each one leads back into

what was first only circle; cut time
is not now so becomes disjointed.
Let those preachers of wood fill air
with backwash or backlash. . . with loss,
loss—are there not incoming
distractions, any *Nebenstimme*?

93

Constantinople, it seems, was packed
up yesterday then mailed out afar.
Little pictures of a city were beat
into one larger one. His desert of jazz
was killingly hot, distance rising out
of horizonless dunes. What became

of that early tribe of musicians in
exit into so-called empty quarters?
Mirages shimmered at his feet; air
just seemed to waver but actually
did waver. There was no life there
unless deep under molten sand.

One going down far beneath may
even find traces of moisture, but
the clavicle of sands will not bend
longer without snapping. Wolves
crest the broad horizon; his sax
will soon dominate the clave.

The Standard Model

The Standard Model will stand as one of humanity's most . . .
profound achievements. . . .
—M. Mangano, SCIENCE 356:1213(2017)

Charm:
Silly, isn't it, all we have is time, but not time for things like stupid
dharma tongs or flowers with petals
and stamens.
Exactly now, with so many out-of-work architects extant, what happened to our
signal, to our old timeless way of building?

> *It is a process which brings order out of nothing*
> *but ourselves; it cannot be attained,*
> *but will happen of its own accord,*
> *if we will only let it.*

What are the stakes in this sanctified game; games of heart, of stasis, games
of lone insects and of leg throbs?

Tau:
Whenever a thing's useful for looking far ahead but still has incompletenesses,
will we ever know what we know
or what we don't; or, out at distant
edges of some c. 1154 paper map, how much is still terra incognita?
Which will come back in the middle of next spring or summer
to bite us on our tender ass. Furthermore,
how many illuminated minds need agree that this is this
and that is that and *No more sass, miss,*
please,
until some smallest, just-forgotten mind up and asks, *Gee,*
what's that tiny, rumpled thing over there in a distant, dark corner?
Is that a jock strap, a knucklebone? So, here's to small, most ignominiously
forgotten things that, like a pet chia lamb,
blossom into gargantuanness with only minimum moisture. A patchwork

quilt,
a tapestry.

W boson:
Those highly sentient scientists, they dig down into strata, throw time
and reputation into wisps. Take crazy gambles, spend extreme hours away
from family,
suffer pains and indignities—and so, let's dig deeper. *No, let sleeping*
dogs lie, says the other side. *Why open up a can of worms; what we have now is*
good enough;
put energy into other areas; it's not going to make the price of our morning
Starbucks drop below 50 cents.

Muon:
Shooting stars, anemones, heat-vent worms, rare viruses, happinesses;
what is the most
important life-thing to you? Preservation, say, of species? What actually
matters in a universe
possibly and unthinkably, even unimaginably, full of alternative species,
taxa, order, and phylum? Love, as in, *All you need is love.*
Let's think
this through—can we ever really know what's best for us?
Prediction is hard, especially about the future. (et sequens, Fidelity Investments
should state, *The future is* not *a good indicator of the past.*)

Higgs:
Pascal's dictum, *The heart has its reasons which reason knows nothing*
notwithstanding, what's the nut here? Do we have to wait for extraterrestrial
intervention
in order to get our messy model-houses in order? Maybe *La Traviata* is the
answer. Maybe a big meteorite incoming. If we were wiped out in a flash,
would it really matter to this warming universe;
maybe we are just a speck in a corner of a cosmos
that has no real bearing
one way or another. R.H. always asked, *What's at the end of the universe,*
that farthest end?

Strange:

Maybe it's a tree somewhere in Tanzania, maybe an Acacia. We love models,
love constructing them;
they offer us security, but recall H.K.'s *Life is either a daring adventure,*
or nothing on same subject, or T.S.E.'s *the world ends / Not with a bang but*
a whimper. Regardless, it ends with *A Boy's Will.* Good question,
what do we get in return for all this
discovery and hard work, I mean, in the cosmic sense? Unfold a binary star,
unfold a gingko leaf—do they not all look the same?

Gluon:

Flicker-lit and half-primitive, see what it means to rely entirely
on a model
that is faulty, even incomplete,
even not knowing what is missing. As Archie wrote, *Hard to see*
the missing from what's not there. Is this evolution perhaps punctuated,
or quite random and unpredictable in the midst of gross predictability, à la old-
school Darwin?
What we don't know we don't know, maybe will never
know. Like dark matter or energy, all we do know is about five percent of our
dank, cornered universe. Like trajectories in art—what has been overlooked or
lost to mind, or in future what will be lost. What could have been
in past or future is a case for *via negativa*, a way of describing
something
by saying what it is not, certainly *not* ultimate reality.

Up:

but a resistance to the dominant narrative; rather like offering another way, like
reticence. Lo, the miracle and my lost feline concerns.
You find that lost something
at the last place
you look,
but why would you stop looking for it at the second-to-last place?

A Community of Whores

A rose's fallen petal, pink as all get-out, paints the *démarche*.
At end of road, at finis, nothing is really necessary;
everything settles out optional—like, leave your quite unstarched
thongs eternally pinned up high on outdoor clotheslines.
They'll still be damp when you get back from therapy group.

Wonder why whores always whine in those semi-anonymous sessions?
Aspens, exotic cashews, sacred *Crateva religiosa* thrive,
transpire, never cry; a plant's personal gain is carbon, water,
sun. Compromised, a tree more than cries—it dies.
That ancient aspen's sole principle—propagation.

No schemes, no stinky published commerce. Nuts in group sessions
mouth all-times, *Everything's Perfect.* That's . . . what, community?
So, you nuts, try this: grab your favorite barnyard
chicken, twirl it tight around a circle, switch back
and snap its neck; then go look at things from that
bird's perspective. Mahalo. May the whirlwinds of fate

lift to send you into the strange province of No-Time.
Overtaken by events, non-nobles and coachmen shiver,
precess, upturn, drive-back. *Write, write like Archie,*
their pathetic bird-brains signal. Their gut-hearts
signal too, to not leave anything to chance.
Perfect, desirable, but . . . inculcatable?

Afterwards, light and dark rose-scents waft.

Window Sitter

—*Madogiwa-zoku,* the window-ledge tribe

Mother Earth sat close by her brightly lit, framed window
that, on its own, spun her tales; its iron frame recycled silent
earth, pushing ancient tales tight against bright, outside light.

She, Mother of all Earth, was unnaturally cold by that window;
felt more and more the cold. Such mornings, when her full
shadow had been round her, she coaxed and sent all her

love back into it. All about her seemed a green, some richer
shade, surprisingly masculine but still hunting. Wrinkled skin
across her arms was both honest but so uninteresting. Not

yet daft, but edging towards—all that sitting in sunlight—
and much of her legacy so gone. Finally, faint water, swift
and unrippled, dark, three times lapped slowly across her

seated chair's circumference. She now felt bereft; her sister
earth-tribes as a whole late-concurred—*For all our good,* those
crusty minders crooned. Presently, a quiet ether spread out

along her still-fertile center, around the window seat, rose up
to keep her company. She rose from her chair now, turned
to move about, but—door was closed, oh no. Still wished to

run back outside, do any work, even pull cancerous weeds. Her
tribes-kin were sourly emotional—she, always the maverick, had
long ago sparked her tribe's deep dismay by baldly eradicating

a whole northern, queer-but-burgeoning, huge-reptilian clan—a
near-final affront to her tribe, that village of modest refinement.
But earth's gross warming had also by then begun; that so cloyed,

they threw ethics, myths, even taboos at her. Thereafter began
her long staring out to open, bluest sky—but, just then, conjured
a new, happy, creative idea: how to redistribute spirit—her own

too, sure, because harmony was so concordant a value. Back then,
in her early management years, she had crafted what grew to be
a golden Eden; crafted it all by twisting numerous manners of art.

She began with a red ball, then green, but her final cloudy-blue—
so like a birthday cake amid hot sparklers. There was, in that
early time, no fear; back then, her hands pressed and molded

air's fabric so facilely. *But today,* she sighed, *it smells just like
tired pond scum. All my team was on board then, all our fates
tied altogether,* she murmured, sitting there by that window,

but no longer. Soon, Mother felt a faint, distant need; someone
or other, somewhere, was waving her back in. She turned
her face to her past for review: *What had worked, what hadn't?*

Did I change, she wondered, *or did it?* There was always the Agency,
they might take her back. But long, hard waves restrained hope,
her final breakwater. She could move about now and so does;

goes out long stretches, but when truth and harmony collide,
truth often gets swept under a rug. That harmony, so highly
refined an emotion, or sensitivity—no absolutism entered in.

She, intensely certain but qualmed a bit, yet not lost: *Silly, silly,
though I can still churn it up like I used to; must speed up a bit
for sure.* Her fingers crook then uncrook, then crook again,

but get warm and straighten out. Nothing then manifested; magic
had evaporated since her old times, had ended. Understanding
her rejection by the collective, she knew, did not cure it; was only

an indefinite help for comprehended nearing darkness. There were no honest conversations anymore. Her tribe-kin, so offended, always rushed to undercut her. To that shelved Mother, an old, cloudy earth

was not obliged to return any loyalty. Its only new need is to create.

And Just This Far from Hopelessness

Every blade of grass is crowned with dew.
Every daffodil raises its spring head anew.

Every heartbeat, a wondrous second chance.
Every lover's nudge, a frothy human dance.

Our clairvoyant world winds beastly or not.
Our ice cream's mint syrup is sticky and hot.

Our cat caught a sad mouse, but just let it go.
Our toes want their socks prepared for snow.

Why swans mate for life, a quite delicate issue.
Why worlds don't collide, a matter for Vishnu.

Why anyone buys annuities—a broker's spite?
Why garage doors spring open as aliens alight?

Every raw Andean gem deserves a perfect cut.
Every under-sink leak reveals a plumber's butt.

Anticline

Tomorrow will be different,
    a man thinks,
so he walks out into the sea
        to watch the curve of placements
      of advancing and retreating sea-tides,
and to close the watchlist and to prepare.
Tomorrow will be very different.

Tomorrow, God will come back to restore order;
    God or someone else will barbeque our steaks.
Then, the newest archangel Uriel
    will stow his knitting in a basket and stand up—
today was the day for Uriel to get everything stowed.
      Uriel will be on the watchlist for the next week or two.

    Look, someone is always, always, on the spot.
Courage at the last moment
    corresponds in some zero hour to a previous placement
      where enigma and fear spark off each other.

But the sea around the man is warm and cuddly, foam-streaked,
    topped off.
Colorful, stock logos, all conceding central religious arguments, skim
    along the sand foredunes
      in between
dead-looking *Ammophila* clumps.

And the man feels pressed by time because he
    has to make that hand-over between noon and dark,
or else Uriel pulls out of the pact and then God gets his hands dirty
    counting dollar bills picked up from sidewalks in the Deep South—
      if He can't hire some temps to do it for Him.

Uriel hands the man out in the middle of heavy surf a banged-up
    hand trowel,
    suggests he dig a shallow hole
    in the sand underfloor
        so he can transplant wildflower roots there to save them from air.

The surging sea gets warmer and more carbonic.
Portuguese men-of-war pass messages back and forth;
        they decide, *No use to do anything*, and disperse back to homes,
    leaving scraps of paper to drift down.

Everyone breaks out on holiday.
A crowded seaside resort absorbs many;
others off to the Atlas Mountains.
The rest sadly to Antarctica to fish.
Everything grinds to stop.

Everyone throws off their circus masks.
Who is who?

What Do Cats Contribute Positively
to Universal Ecology?

Still as a coconut palm in startled winter
they muster, hiss, stretch; theirs is the world.
An ear in the paw, tail about an inch shorter;
canines sharp and viciously marshmallowed.

Often times seemingly lazy as drunken ants,
conscripted by vile natures into endless sleep.
Fortune-tellers by night, their narrow eye-slits.
So not careful when they kill, leaving heaps

of tails and feathers, bird guts strewn on new divans.
Well then, throw a dry cat out into quite pelting rain;
does it look up in wonder at the hydrologic cycle?
No, it hauls ass to nearby porticos, to any open bible.

Well, *do* cats contribute positively to universal ecology?
Oh no, settled down in fur, they punctuate astrology.

Underworld Children

Some tremble with cold,
even bunched tight together.
Inside, folded under stiff
transparent sleeves,
they link hands. A moon
is a concept in midair
they think they know,
but no wisdom is their own.

Show us beetles, their insistent, tinny chorus.
Beetles! Old ants! To annoy,
they snap fingernails together
to throw sparks. On the longest day
they skate fjords, and on that day
the blessed from the centermost
island carry warmth out
to them in rucksacks.

The Woman Who Never Slept

Letter in hand, out into dankness. Plants blue corn-
tufts, paints all fresh breeze off the upper slopes.
Halcyon clouds twist a ponderously thick unicorn
into a wrecking ball, next a hackneyed jump rope.

Underneath currents, against little oceans, at night
navigating by stars, she swims on her ancient back
to corral dizzying right whales. Incredibly bright
at nearly ninety, every midnight channels Dirac

to downshift a hot, quivering mind to be still.
Endearingly Hermes-like, shuttles along
borders, walking straight a hundred quadrilles
on callused bare toes; quite reviles a hexameron.

Village chickens, donkeys announce her annunciation—
startled back to life, hands odd letter to headsmen.

Notes

"A Bee in Late October": The Greeks believed that a baby whose lips were touched by a bee would become a great poet or speaker (from *Legends and Lore of Bees*, ThoughtCo).

"A Community of Whores": "No-Time" is a saying by Amrit Sorli.

"A Shark Is Not": $M\odot$ is the astrophysical symbol for one solar mass. Trinity was the code name of the first detonation of a nuclear weapon.

"A Verso Likeness (Imagined, Of Course) of Some Acquaintances: A Childless, Wanting Couple in Aberdeen, WA, with Doubt like Water": Nicholas Negroponte is an American architect.

"Amour in the Age of Viruses, Porcupines, of Immunology": *Hathor, Urania*, and *Melpomene*: the Muses. "Interestingly, porcupines, unique among mammals, carry immunogens that work by 'priming' the human immune system against existential retroviruses." (from "Porcine Endogenous Retrovirus in Xenotransplantation," Clive Patience)

"At the Self-Serve": *Ununnilium*, element 110, now named *Darmstadtium*.

"Black Dirt": *Krell* and *Altair IV* are from the classic 1956 science fiction film *The Forbidden Planet*.

"Eridanus, Mythical River": *Eridanus*, also known as *The River*, is a southern constellation. The *Acheron* is the fabled principal river of Hades. *Actaeon*, from Greek mythology, is also known as *The Hunter* (Wikipedia).

"Final Canticle, on the Tools for Cultivation of Our Own Secret Garden": *Transeunt* is defined as a mental act producing an effect outside of the mind.

"Hive": Based on T. H. White's tetralogy, *The Once and Future King*.

"In a Hostage Situation: A Play in Four Acts": *Grasshopper* is a reference from Philip K. Dick's *The Man in the High Castle*.

"Invasive Species": "The Evolutionary Impact of Invasive Species and the Indirect Evolutionary Consequences of Mixing," H. A. Mooney and E. E. Cleland. *Sarowar*, from *The Land of the Gurkhas or The Himalayan Kingdom of Nepal*, by William Brook Northey.

"Inventing a New Color": I believe it may be physically impossible to actually invent a new color, although the electromagnetic spectrum is pretty wide: before ELF to beyond HX.

"Male Sperm Counts Are Falling All Across the Western World": "Countdown: Yet another study suggests sperm numbers are falling in rich countries," *The Economist*, Dec 8th, 2012.

"My Heart's Gone Uzi": *Zeno's Paradox* is a problem not with finding the sum, but rather with finishing a task with an infinite number of steps: how can one ever get from A to B, if there are an infinite number of (non-instantaneous) events possible between the two points?

"My Transuranium Goblet": The Pakistani A. Q. Khan is a reviled master of nuclear proliferation. "The trick is told when the trick is sold" is either from the film *The Grifters* or the film *House of Games*.

"On Online Dating": Sir Ernest Shackleton placed such an ad in the London newspaper *The Times* to seek recruits for his 1914 Imperial Trans-Antarctic Expedition.

"Strait of Georgia": The hyphenate word *wave-doors* is from Mary Oliver's poem "Bone." *Aokigahara*, also known as "The Sea of Trees," is a forest on the northwestern flank of Japan's Mount Fuji. This forest has an historical reputation as home to *yurei* (ghosts of the dead in Japanese mythology). In recent years, Aokigahara has become internationally known as "The Suicide Forest," one of the world's most prevalent suicide sites." (from Wikipedia).

"*Symmetry*": "XVII. Architecture of a human brain . . . ." from "The architecture of functional lateralisation and its relationship to callosal connectivity in the human brain," Karolis, Corbetta, and de Schotten, in *Nature Communications*.

"The Literal Mind Was Crushed": Sergei Pavlovich Diaghilev was a Russian art critic, patron, ballet impresario and a founder of the *Ballets Russes*. This poem was inspired in part by the Russian Futurist opera *Victory over the Sun*, which premiered in 1913 at the Luna Park in Saint Petersburg, and which I saw one evening in Spain around 1980.

"The Orb Weaver": The *Oort Cloud*, named after the Dutch astronomer Jan Oort, is a theoretical cloud of predominantly icy planetesimals proposed to surround the Sun. *The Time Machine* is a science fiction novella by H. G. Wells; see for *Morlocks, Weena, A.D. 802,701,* and *George,* the English scientist.

"The Standard Model": The *Standard Model* of particle physics is a theory describing three of the four known fundamental forces (the electromagnetic, weak, and strong interactions, but not including the gravitational force) in the universe, as well as classifying all known elementary particles. *Charm, Tau,* etc., are the elementary particles of the Standard Model. *R.H.* is Robert Heinlein, the science-fiction writer; *H.K.* is Helen Keller, the author; *T.S.E.* is T. S. Eliot; *Archie* is A.R. Ammons. *A Boy's Will* is Robert Frost's first published book of poems.

"The Woman Who Never Slept": Paul Dirac was a mathematician who won the Nobel Prize. Hermes is considered a god of transitions and boundaries. The word *hexameron* describes God's work on the six days of creation, or is a reference to the six days of creation themselves. The woman in the poem is modelled after the old woman I encountered on many nights as a teenager, driving my 1945 Willys jeep along dirt roads in Colombia; she was an insomniac, employed to carry messages from village to village.

"Treechild": *Yggdrasil* is a huge mythical tree that connects the nine worlds in Norse mythology. *Mimisbrunnr,* from the same source.

"Trophy": Refer to the cartoon in The New Yorker, December 13th, 1999, on page 88.

"Voluntarism:: Form and tone suggested by Robert Frost's blank-verse poem "Home Burial."

"Window Sitter": The term refers to a worker phenomenon in Japan as described in the online article "Unneeded Workers In Japan Are Bored, And Very Well Paid" at URL: www2.shizuokanet.ne.jp/sabu/window.html.

About the Author

R. J. Keeler was born in St. Paul, Minnesota, and grew up in the jungles of Colombia. He holds a BS in Mathematics from North Carolina State University, an MS in Computer Science from the University of North Carolina-Chapel Hill, an MBA from University of California at Los Angeles, and a Certificate in Poetry from the University of Washington. An Honorman in the U.S. Naval Submarine School, he was Submarine Service (SS) qualified. He is a recipient of the Vietnam Service Medal, Honorable Discharge, and a Whiting Foundation Experimental Grant. He is a member of IEEE (technological society), AAAS (scientific society), and the Academy of American Poets. A former Boeing engineer.

CPSIA information can be obtained
at www.ICGtesting.com
Printed in the USA
FSHW010146050220
66705FS